Accidental Genius

Science Puzzles for Clever

S	L	H	K	Z	H	C	Y	H	E
L	U	P	D	S	U	B	O	L	C
Q	S	N	R	V	M	X	R	L	R
P	I	K	S	T	I	R	S	V	D
W	S	M	T	H	D	P	N	I	T
Q	D	R	V	M					
R									

SUNSHINE, HURRICANES, BLIZZARDS, and RAINBOWS

Weather Science

Alix Wood

WINDMILL BOOKS

Photocopy, print, or trace the puzzles if you are sharing this book with others. Then you won't spoil the book for the next person.

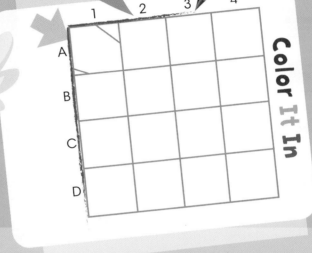

Published in 2024 by Windmill Books,
an Imprint of Rosen Publishing
2544 Clinton Street
Buffalo, NY 14224

Written, designed, and illustrated by Alix Wood
All other images © AdobeStock Images

Cataloging-in-Publication Data

Names: Wood, Alix.
Title: Sunshine, hurricanes, blizzards, and rainbows / Alix Wood.
Description: Buffalo, New York : Windmill Books, 2024. |
Series: Accidental genius: science puzzles for clever kids |
Identifiers: ISBN 9781538395257 (pbk.) | ISBN 9781538395264 (library bound) | ISBN 9781538395271 (ebook)
Subjects: LCSH: Weather--Juvenile literature. | Games--Juvenile literature. | Picture puzzles--Juvenile literature.
Classification: LCC QC981.3 W66 2024 | DDC 551.5--dc23

Printed in the United States of America

CPSIA Compliance Information: Batch #CW24WM
For Further Information contact Rosen Publishing at 1-800-237-9932

Find us on

Contents

What Is Weather?

Why do we wear a T-shirt some days, but need a warm coat on other days? Because the weather changes. Weather is the way the air around us feels. It is how hot, cold, cloudy, snowy, rainy, or windy it is each day.

The Main Weather Elements

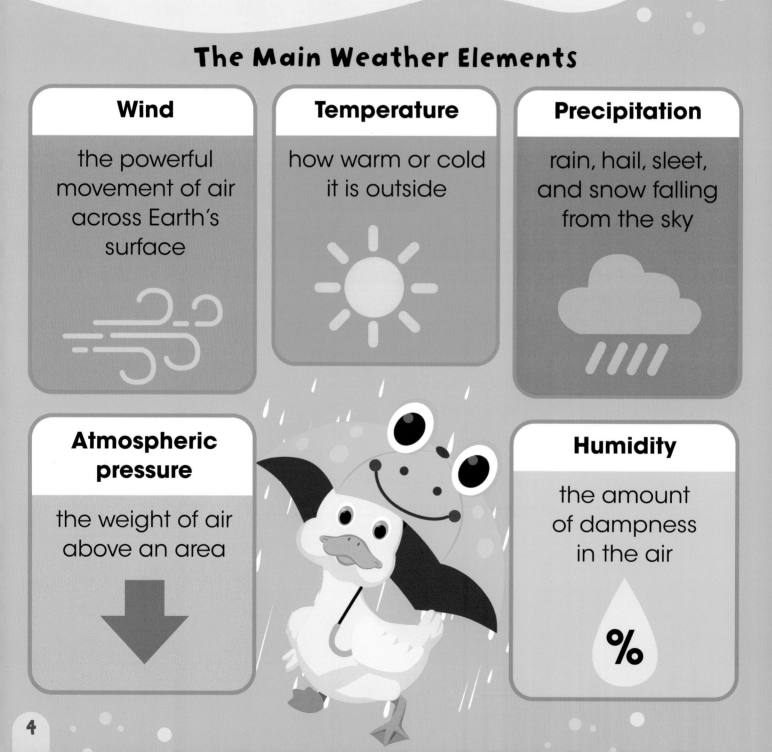

Wind

the powerful movement of air across Earth's surface

Temperature

how warm or cold it is outside

Precipitation

rain, hail, sleet, and snow falling from the sky

Atmospheric pressure

the weight of air above an area

Humidity

the amount of dampness in the air

%

Picture Match

Can you find the 4 pictures showing precipitation?

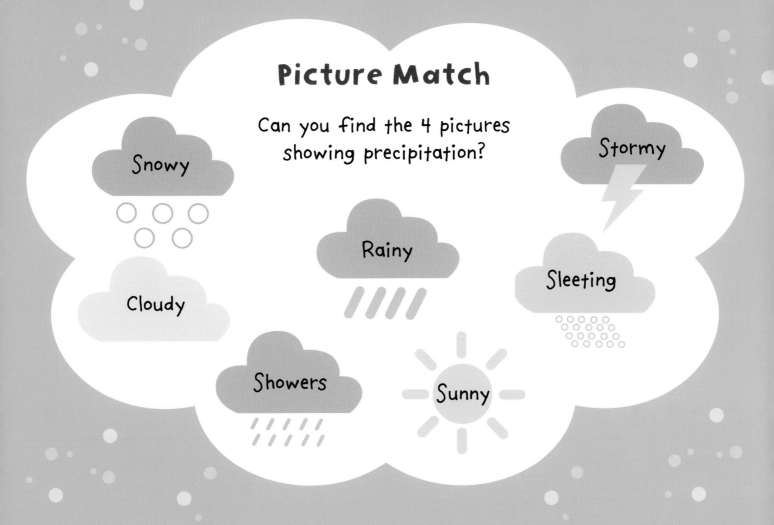

Snowy

Stormy

Rainy

Sleeting

Cloudy

Showers

Sunny

Word Search

Can you find the 9 weather words below?

S	L	H	K	Z	H	C	Y	H	E
L	U	P	D	S	U	B	O	L	C
Q	S	N	R	V	M	X	R	L	R
P	I	K	S	T	I	R	S	V	D
W	S	M	T	H	D	P	N	I	T
Q	D	R	V	M	I	F	O	W	E
R	C	A	E	W	T	N	W	R	E
N	S	W	M	L	Y	Z	E	G	L
X	R	A	I	N	E	V	O	L	S
P	R	E	S	S	U	R	E	P	X

RAIN
WIND
SLEET
SUNSHINE
HUMIDITY
WARM
COLD
PRESSURE
SNOW

Chart Your Weather

What's the weather like where you live? Does it change every day, or every week? Try making a weather chart. It is a great way to record the changes in your area.

Make a Weather Chart

On a large sheet of paper, draw eight vertical lines, 2 inches (5 cm) apart.

Write the days of the week along the top of your chart.

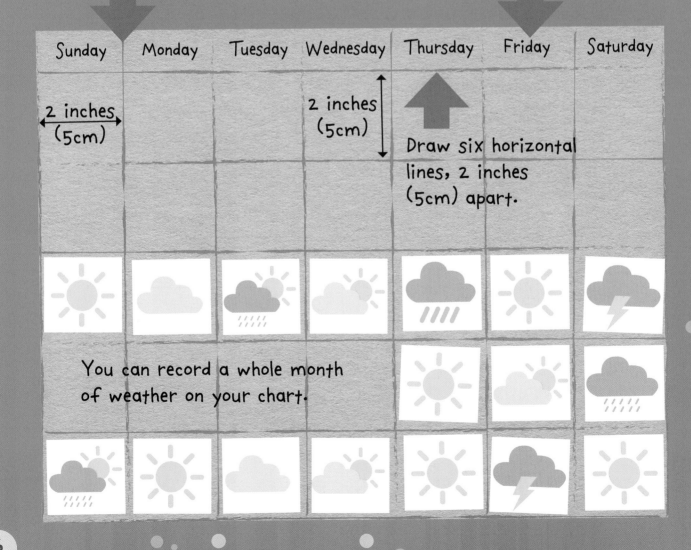

Sunday	Monday	Tuesday	Wednesday	Thursday	Friday	Saturday

2 inches (5cm)

2 inches (5cm)

Draw six horizontal lines, 2 inches (5cm) apart.

You can record a whole month of weather on your chart.

Trace these weather pictures onto squares of paper. Then use them on your chart. You may need several of each common weather type.

sunny

partly sunny

cloudy

showers

rain

thunderstorms

snowy

windy

icy

sleet

Could you be a weather forecaster? Predict the weather for the next day on your chart. Then see if you were right!

Weather Forecasts

Scientists studying the weather can predict what the weather will be like. Can you help Duck with his weather forecast below? Read the weather report. Then match the weather symbols to the right places on the map.

And here is the weather ...
- It will be sunny in Africa and South America.
- Snow will fall in Asia for most of the day.
- It will rain in North America.
- Clouds will cover Australia until next week.

High Tech ...

Weather scientists are called meteorologists. Meteorologists use weather satellites to measure and forecast the weather.

Satellites are sent into space on rockets. Once there, they get a great view of the weather happening over Earth. They track cloud patterns and changes in temperature.

... and Low Tech

You can forecast the weather using a pine cone! Pine cones are full of tiny seeds. The cones open up on dry days, and the wind carries the seeds away.

On damp days, the damp seeds are less likely to get carried by the wind. So, the clever pine cones close up.

damp weather

dry weather

The Four Seasons

Our spinning Earth takes a year to travel around the sun. Did you know the Earth spins slightly on its side? So, different parts of the world lean toward the sun more at some times of the year. That's why we get different seasons!

During one part of the year, the countries on the top half of Earth lean toward the sun. They get more hours of sunlight, so it is summer there.

the sun

The countries in the lower half get less sunlight, so it is winter there.

At the opposite time of the year, the lower half leans toward the sun. That's when it's summer there!

Each season lasts three months. Winter can be snowy and cold. Flowers start to bloom in spring. Summer is usually sunny. It gets colder in fall, and leaves and apples fall from the trees.

Can you match each picture to the season?

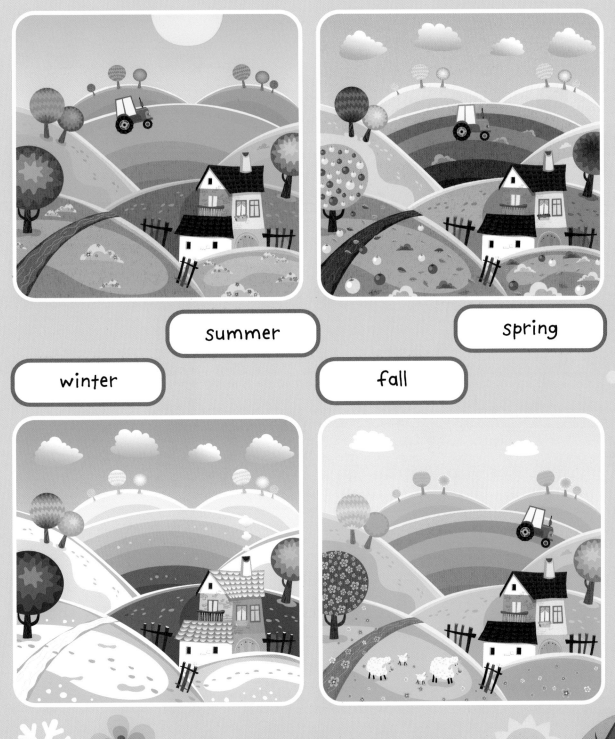

summer

spring

winter

fall

Which season do you like best?

Rainy Days

Rain is water that falls from the sky in drops. People, animals, and plants rely on the water it brings. Rain fills our lakes, ponds, rivers, and streams. If too much rain falls, it can cause dangerous floods.

The village of Mawsynram in northeastern India is the rainiest place on Earth! Most of its rain falls during the summer monsoon.

DID YOU KNOW?
A monsoon is actually a change of wind direction. It can cause heavy rain.

Other places get hardly any rain. The driest place on Earth is the Atacama Desert in Chile. It hasn't rained in some parts of this desert for hundreds of years!

People who study weather are called meteorologists. Meteorologists use special equipment to measure the weather. To measure rainfall, they use an instrument called a rain gauge.

Make Your Own Rain Gauge

You will need: a plastic bottle, scissors, ruler, tape, a marker, some modeling clay, adult help

1. Ask an adult to help carefully cut the top off the bottle. You will need the bottle top later.

2. Press modeling clay into the base of the bottle. This keeps the bottle from tipping over and fills in any dips. Make the top of the clay level. Place the top upside down in your bottle base, to act as a funnel.

3. Using the ruler and a marker, measure and mark the inches or centimeters from the layer of clay up the bottle.

4. Place the bottle outside. Record how much rain you get every day. Remember to empty the gauge after each day's reading.

The Water Cycle

Have you ever wondered where rain comes from? Rain is part of our planet's endless water cycle.

1.
Sunlight heats water on Earth's surface. The heat turns the water into vapor. The vapor rises into the air.

2.
As the vapor cools, it turns back into droplets of water.

3.
The droplets form clouds.

4.
Eventually, the droplets become too heavy to stay in the cloud. They fall as rain.

5.
Then the water cycle begins again.

Make a Water Cycle in a Bowl!

You will need: adult help, a large bowl, a small bowl, hot water, salt, ice cubes, cling wrap

1. Place the small bowl in the center of the large bowl.

2. Ask an adult to pour hot water into the large bowl. Mix in 2 teaspoons of salt. Make sure the water level stays below the lip of the small bowl.

3. Cover the large bowl with cling wrap. Place a handful of ice cubes in the center of the cling wrap. Place the bowl in a sunny place and watch what happens.

The hot water vapor should rise, and then be cooled by the ice. Any droplets will rain into the small bowl. The heavier salt will stay in the large bowl. Taste the water. Is it salty?

A dinosaur might have paddled in the water you drank today! The water cycle has cleaned and recycled the same water for millions of years.

Cool Clouds

Next time you are outside, look up at the clouds. They can tell you a lot about the weather. We see high, wispy clouds in nice weather. A sky full of big, gray clouds means it might rain or snow. Clouds look gray when they are full of water.

Different Types of Clouds

cumulonimbus

cirrus

High in the sky, cirrus clouds are thin and wispy, and often seen on sunny days.

cumulus

Cumulus clouds are white, puffy clouds. They usually mean good weather.

stratus

Stratus clouds form a flat layer, low in the sky. They can bring rain.

Cumulonimbus clouds are very tall. They can bring thunderstorms, heavy rain, hail, and even tornadoes.

Are You a Cloud Expert?

Can you match each cloud to the weather it might bring?

rain

thunderstorms

sunny

Cloud-watching is fun. Have you ever seen clouds form cool shapes in the sky? Try it. Sometimes clouds can look like animals or faces!

Why Does It Thunder?

Thunderstorms happen mostly in summer. Hot, damp air rises quickly and forms thunder clouds. Flashes of lightning heat the air in the clouds. The clouds expand and contract (get bigger and smaller) as they heat and cool. That is what causes the sound of thunder!

rumble

rumble

The thunder and lightning happen at the same time. Sound travels slower than light, so you see the lightning before you hear the thunder.

How Far Away Is a Storm?

It takes the sound of thunder about 5 seconds to travel a mile (1.6 km). To tell how far away a storm is, count the seconds between a flash of lightning and the sound of thunder.

0 seconds = storm is very close
5 seconds = storm is 1 mile (1.6 km) away
15 seconds = storm is 3 miles (4.8 km) away

It's exciting to watch a thunderstorm. But remember, lightning is dangerous. Head indoors to stay safe. Lightning usually strikes the tallest objects and can travel easily through water and metal, so ...

... **DON'T**
- stand in the open or on high ground
- go near trees or tall objects
- go in any water
- fly a kite or hold anything metal

Color It In

Copy this picture and then color it in if you are sharing this book.

Snowflakes

On cold days, water can freeze into ice crystals in the clouds. For it to snow instead of rain, the temperature in the sky must be a freezing 32 degrees Fahrenheit (0 degrees Celsius) or lower. Each snowflake is made up of around 200 frozen ice crystals.

As snowflakes fall, they meet different conditions, which shape how they look. They can form many different, beautiful shapes.

Snowflake Match

Can you find the four matching pairs of snowflakes?

Symmetrical Snowflakes

Something is symmetrical when one half is a mirror image of the other half. Can you draw the missing half of this snowflake? Copy this page first if you're sharing this book.

Want to know a quick way to see the whole snowflake? Try placing a small mirror along this dotted line!

Snowy Days

Do you love the snow? In most countries, snow falls mainly during winter. Warm countries may only get snow on top of tall mountains. The North and South Poles have snow on the ground all year, because they get the least direct sunlight as Earth spins.

North Pole

South Pole

There are so many fun things to do in the snow. Check off each activity as you find it in the picture:

- ☐ skiing
- ☐ having a snowball fight
- ☐ sledding
- ☐ making a snowman
- ☐ ice-skating
- ☐ making a snow angel

Make Your Own Frost!

You will need: a clean and empty can, some crushed ice, water, salt, a paper towel, a magnifying glass

Frost is a thin layer of ice on a surface. It forms when moist air meets a freezing surface. Place a can on a damp paper towel. Half fill the can with ice. Add a tablespoon of cold water. Sprinkle a tablespoon of salt on top. Salt lowers the melting point of ice. Watch and wait as the frost starts to form.

If you have a magnifying glass, take a close look at the frost. Can you see snowflake-like ice crystals?

Hail and Blizzards

Winter weather can be harsh. Have you ever been caught in a hailstorm or a blizzard? Hailstones are balls of ice that fall from the sky. They can be as large as a golf ball! Blizzards are powerful snowstorms that can blow snow into deep piles.

Hail forms in thunderclouds. Water at the top of the tall cloud freezes. The hailstones get bigger as they get coated with more and more ice. Eventually they get so big the cloud cannot hold them, and they fall to Earth.

Blizzards are caused by low temperatures, strong winds, and lots of snow. The wind blows falling snow, and lifts and moves snow already on the ground. Blizzards can make it difficult to see.

Connect the Dots

What is hidden by this snowy blizzard?

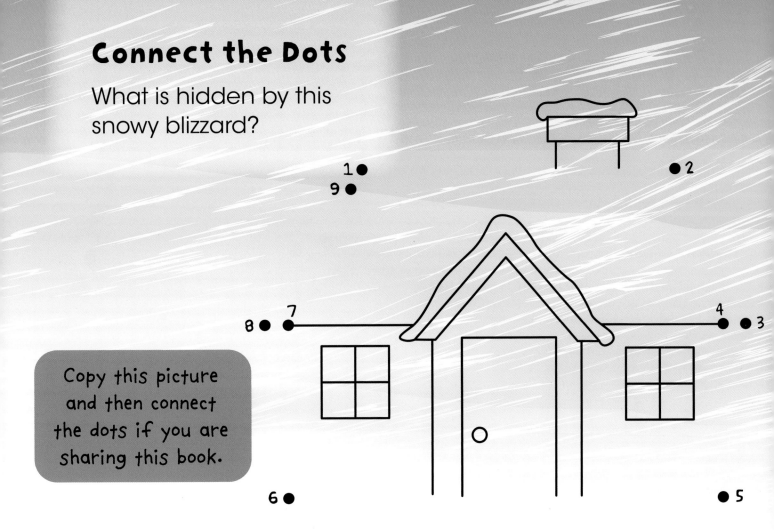

Copy this picture and then connect the dots if you are sharing this book.

Word Search

Can you find the 8 winter words?

FROST
SKIING
BLIZZARD
SNOWMAN
SLEET
HAIL
ICE
SKATING

B	L	G	K	F	S	C	Y	K	H
G	L	N	Z	U	N	B	O	A	C
Q	I	I	R	F	O	L	I	L	R
P	I	I	Z	W	W	L	S	V	D
T	S	K	J	Z	M	P	N	I	T
S	D	S	V	E	A	F	M	C	I
O	C	A	E	R	N	R	W	E	K
R	S	W	M	L	Y	Q	D	G	L
F	R	S	L	E	E	T	U	L	S
P	S	K	A	T	I	N	G	P	X

Windy Weather

Do you like windy days? A gentle breeze can be nice and cooling. Strong winds can blow things around! It is often windy near the ocean or large lakes. Why? Because wind is caused by changes in temperature and air pressure.

Why Does Wind Blow?

Air heats up and rises over a warm surface. Cool air blows into the space left by the rising warm air.

Warm air over the land rises.

Cooler air over the water blows toward the land.

Land heats and cools faster than water.

At night, land cools faster than water. The air over the water is now warmer. So, the wind changes direction and blows toward the ocean or lake.

Are You a Wind Expert?

Write your answers to these three questions on a separate sheet of paper.

1. Match the wind direction arrow to the pictures.

Night

a

b

Day

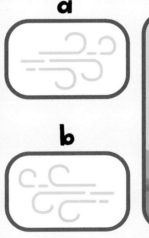

2. What do you call weather where you get wind and snow?

    a) a blizzard   b) a thunderstorm   c) a shower

3. Unscramble these letters to make three types of wind.

T N
D O R
O A

L G
E A

R E
E E
B Z

_ _ _ _ _ _ _ _   _ _ _ _   _ _ _ _ _ _

Using the Wind

We can use the power of the wind to help us get around. Sailboats rely on wind to travel across oceans. Engineless airplanes, called gliders, use rising air to help them stay in the sky.

a glider

Wonderful Windsocks

Have you ever seen a stripy windsock at an airport? Its stripes aren't just for decoration. The angle of the windsock helps show the speed of the wind. Wind can be measured in knots. Each wind-filled stripe on the windsock equals 3 knots of wind speed.

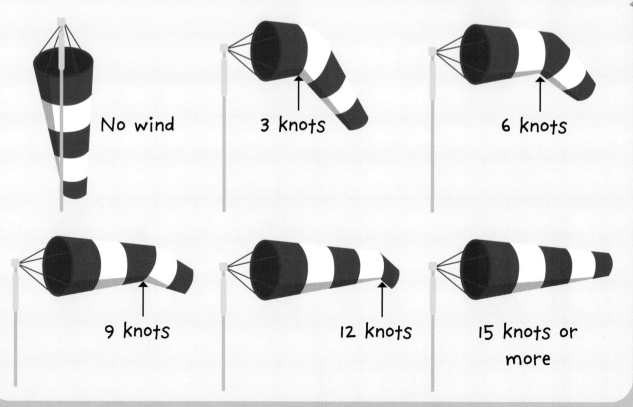

No wind

3 knots

6 knots

9 knots

12 knots

15 knots or more

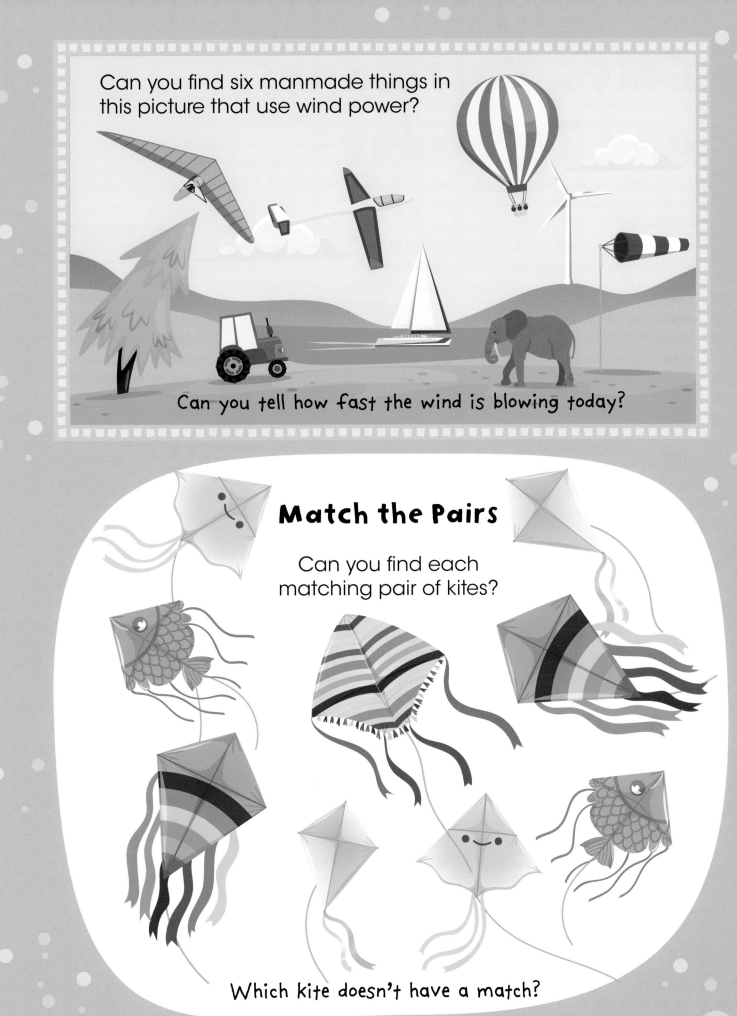

Can you find six manmade things in this picture that use wind power?

Can you tell how fast the wind is blowing today?

Match the Pairs

Can you find each matching pair of kites?

Which kite doesn't have a match?

Gales, Hurricanes, and Tornadoes

Different types of strong winds have special names, such as gales, hurricanes, and tornadoes.

A gale is a very strong wind.

Hurricanes can be more than 1,000 miles (1,609 km) across!

Hurricanes, cyclones, and typhoons are swirling storms that form over warm water. They have different names depending on where in the world they form.

A tornado is a swirling, funnel-shaped cloud that forms under thunderclouds. Wind speeds inside tornadoes can reach 250 miles (402 km) per hour!

Measure Wind Speed with a Wind Gauge

You will need: some cardstock, string, a paper clip, tape, scissors, hole punch, pen, ruler, paper, a glue stick

1. Trace this picture onto paper and glue it to some cardstock.

2. Punch a hole at the red dot.

3. Tie a paper clip to one end of the string. Thread the other end through the hole from front to back. Allow enough string so the paper clip can swing and point to the numbers. Then, tape the string in place at the back.

4. Hold your gauge so the paperclip points to 0. Point the arrow toward the wind. The number your paper clip points to is your wind speed.

Hurricanes rotate counterclockwise north of the equator and clockwise south of the equator!

equator

Sunshine

The sun is the closest star to Earth. It gives us heat and light. Life on Earth could not exist without it. The sun may be our closest star, but it is still a long way away. It takes 8 minutes and 20 seconds for the light leaving the sun to reach Earth!

Sun Clock

You can tell what time of day it is by looking for the sun. As Earth spins, the sun rises in the east and sets in the west.

west

east

When the sun is high in the sky, it is around midday.

When the sun is low in the west, it is evening.

Never look directly at the sun. It can damage your eyes.

If the sun is low in the sky in the east, it must be early morning.

Find out which direction is east and which is west. Then try it yourself.

The sun helps everything on the farm grow.
Can you find these animals and vegetables in the picture?

1 cow   2 pumpkins   3 sheep   4 ducklings   5 turnips

Color It In

Copy this picture and then color it in if you are sharing this book.

Colorful Rainbows

Rainbows are so beautiful. They happen when the sun shines through water in the air. Rainbows can be seen on sunny, rainy days. They can also be seen if it is misty or foggy. If there are water drops in the air and light shining from behind at the right angle, you will see a rainbow.

Light bends and slows down as it passes through water. Light is made up of different colors. Each color of light bends at a different angle, so you see each color separately!

If you saw a rainbow from high in the sky, you'd see a giant circle. From the ground, we can only see half the circle!

Make Your Own Magical Rainbow!

You will need: a sunny day, an outdoor space, a garden hose attached to a faucet

1. Stand with your back to the sun.

2. Place your thumb over the end of the hose to create a spray. Watch out, you may get wet!

3. Rainbows show up best against a dark background, such as a hedge or wall.

Did you see a rainbow?

Do you know the colors of a rainbow?
Color this rainbow in to find out.

1 = red
2 = orange
3 = yellow
4 = green
5 = blue
6 = indigo
7 = violet

Color It In

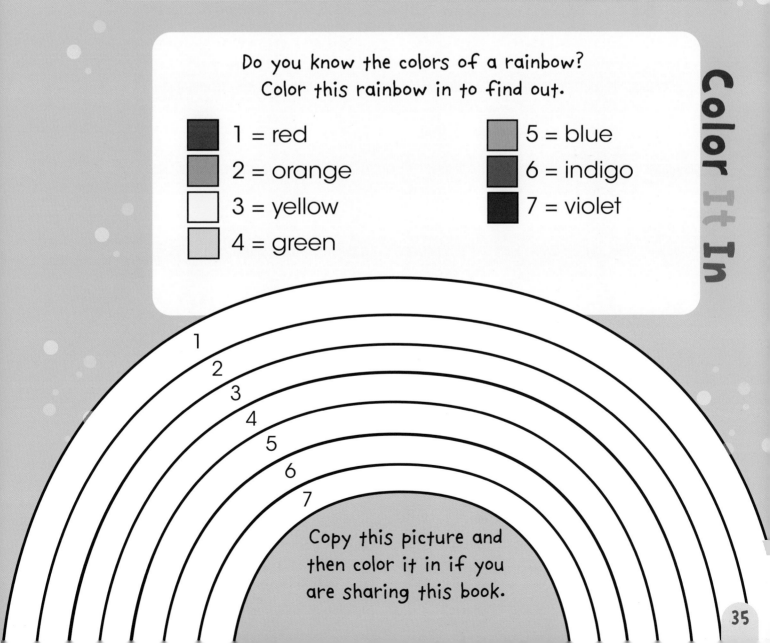

1
2
3
4
5
6
7

Copy this picture and then color it in if you are sharing this book.

Hot Days, Cold Days

Different things affect how hot or cold it is where we live. For example, the way Earth spins around the sun causes places to be hot or cold.

North Pole

The chilly North and South Poles get the least direct sunlight.

Oceans heat up and cool down slower than land does. The warm sea keeps coastal places warmer in winter.

Places near the equator are hot because they get the most direct sun.

South Pole

It is colder on a mountain than at sea level. The air is thinner there and less able to store heat.

Wind can make air feel cool. The direction the wind is coming from can bring icy or warm air.

Winds are named after the direction they come from. Wind blowing from west to east is called a westerly.

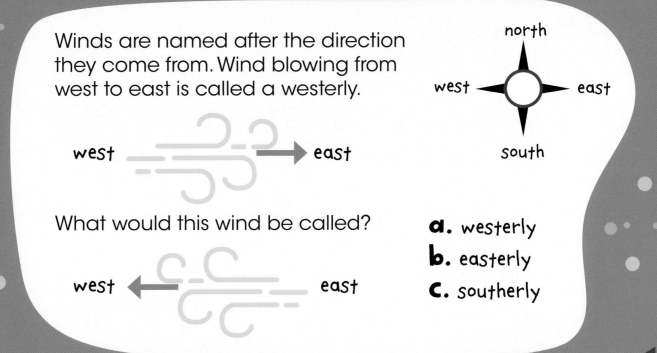

west ———→ east

What would this wind be called?

west ←——— east

a. westerly

b. easterly

c. southerly

Make a Weather Vane

You will need: modeling clay, a square of cardstock, pencil with an eraser, pin, drinking straw, scissors, construction paper, marker, compass, adult to help you

1. Find north using a compass. Draw a cross on the card stock. Mark north, south, east, and west.

2. Snip a notch in each end of the straw.

3. Cut an arrow and tail shape out of construction paper. Slide them into the slits on the straw.

4. Place modeling clay in the center of your square. Push the tip of the pencil into the clay.

5. Ask an adult to help you push a pin through the center of the straw, into the eraser. Make sure the straw spins easily.

The arrow will point to the direction the wind is blowing.

Sun Protection

A thin layer of gases around Earth helps protect it from getting too hot or too cold. Imagine you are the sun's rays. Use your finger to find your way through the gassy atmosphere to reach Earth.

Climate Change

Weather scientists have noticed that Earth is getting warmer. The gases around Earth trap heat, a little like the glass walls of a greenhouse. The trapped heat makes Earth warm enough to live on. But destroying forests and burning fuel creates more greenhouse gases. This makes Earth get too warm, too fast.

Which things will help protect you from the sun's rays?

Fog and Ice

Fog is a cloud that forms near the ground. It forms when water vapor gathers around bits of dust in the air. Sea fog forms around bits of sea salt in the water vapor. Fog is common in valleys and near water. It usually forms at night, as the air cools. When the sun comes out, the fog dries up.

Make Fog in a Jar!

You will need: hot tap water, a jar with a lid, hairspray, ice cubes

1. Fill the jar with hot tap water. Then pour away half the water.

2. Turn the jar lid upside down and fill it with ice cubes.

3. Spray a tiny squirt of hairspray into the jar. Balance the upside-down jar lid on the jar.

4. Watch the foggy cloud form.

What's happening? The hairspray provides dust particles for the fog to form around. The ice cubes cool the vapor to form a fog-like cloud.

Ice is frozen water. Water in ponds and lakes can freeze in cold weather. Sliding on the ice can be fun—but NEVER walk or skate on a frozen lake or pond. The ice might break and you could fall into dangerously cold water.

Duck is skating around an ice rink. Can you follow his trail and find where he skated from?

Why Is Sunset Colorful?

Light contains all the different colors of the rainbow. When the colors mix together, they create a white light. Gases in the air cause the light to scatter. The color blue gets scattered the most, so in daytime, a clear sky appears blue.

At sunset and sunrise, the sun is lower in the sky. The low angle causes other colors to get scattered more.

As the light fades, you may see black outlines of objects against the setting sun. These outlines are called silhouettes.

Can you match each animal to its silhouette?

Draw a Sunset

Copy the drawing in each square into the correct square in the grid below.

A 1 A 2 A3 A4 B 1

B 2 B 3 B4 C1 C2

C3 C 4

Trace the grid onto some paper if you are sharing this book.

We have filled in the first square for you.

	1	2	3	4
A				
B				
C				

Color It In

Weather Genius Test

Are you a weather genius? Answer these questions to find out.

1 What is precipitation?

a) rain, snow, and hail

b) tornadoes, gales, and hurricanes

2 Is it colder or warmer on a mountain?

a) It is colder because the air is thinner.

b) It is warmer because it is closer to the sun.

3

What is this type of cloud called?

a) cirrus b) stratus c) cumulus

4 Why do we get seasons?

a) Because the sun sets at night.

b) Different parts of Earth tilt toward the sun at different times of year.

c) Because summer makes everyone happy.

5 In summer, what should you wear to protect yourself from the sun?

a) a big coat, scarf, and a wooly hat

b) a swimsuit

c) a hat, sunscreen, and sunglasses

6 During a thunderstorm, why do you see the lightning before you hear thunder?

a) Because the light is really bright.

b) Because light travels faster than sound.

c) Because thunder happens later.

Answers

Page 5:

S	L	H	K	Z	H	G	Y	H	E
L	U	P	D	S	U	B	O	L	C
Q	S	M	R	V	M	X	R	L	R
P	I	K	S	T	I	R	S	V	D
W	S	M	T	H	D	P	N	I	T
Q	D	R	V	M	F	O	W	E
R	C	A	E	W	T	I	W	R	E
N	S	W	M	L	Y	Z	E	G	L
X	R	A	I	N	E	V	O	L	S
P	R	E	S	S	U	R	E	P	X

Page 8:

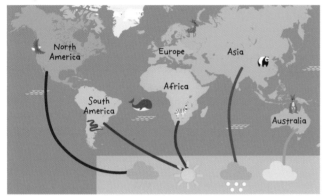

Page 11: 1) a 2) c 3) d 4) b

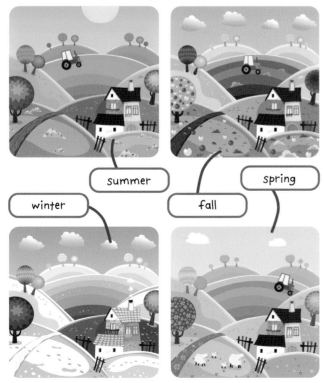

summer

winter

fall

spring

Page 17:

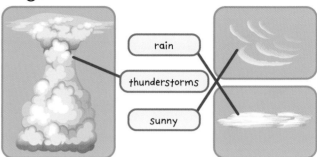

rain

thunderstorms

sunny

Page 20:

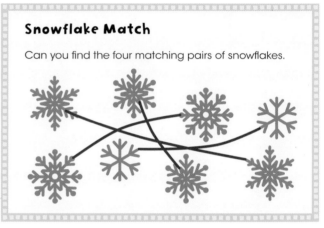

Snowflake Match

Can you find the four matching pairs of snowflakes.

Page 21: The whole snowflake looks like this.